7 Keys

to a Winning CV

How to create a CV that gets results

By Mildred Talabi

HARRIMAN HOUSE LTD

3A Penns Road
Petersfield
Hampshire
GU32 2EW
GREAT BRITAIN

Tel: +44 (0)1730 233870
Fax: +44 (0)1730 233880
Email: enquiries@harriman-house.com
Website: www.harriman-house.com

First published in Great Britain in 2011

ISBN: 978-0-85719-158-8

British Library Cataloguing in Publication Data
A CIP catalogue record for this book can be obtained from the British Library.

Printed and bound in the UK by CPI Group (UK) Ltd, Croydon, CR0 4YY.

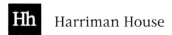 Harriman House

I dedicate this book to anyone who desires to have a fulfilling and enjoyable work life – life is too short to do otherwise.

Contents

About the author

Mildred Talabi is an award-winning businesswoman, trained journalist and editor. Her venture into CV writing began in 2006 when she left her role as assistant editor of a film magazine to set up her own CV consultancy in response to the market need. Since then, Mildred has carried out numerous CV makeovers and one-to-one review sessions, and delivered CV seminars and workshops to hundreds of people.

Mildred is passionate about helping people attain enjoyable and fulfilling work lives and attributes her own career satisfaction to having always pursued her passion – whatever that may be at the time – and developing the ability to write effective CVs, cover letters and job application forms.

To find out more about Mildred, please visit **www.mildredtalabi.com**.

Seminars and speaking engagements

If you would like to enquire about booking Mildred for a CV seminar or a work-related speaking engagement at your organisation, please email **info@mildredtalabi.com**.

Feedback and testimonials

Please email all feedback and CV success testimonials as a result of using this book to **7keys@mildredtalabi.com**.

Acknowledgements

My first acknowledgement and thanks is to JC – my best friend, chief encourager and the one who enabled me to write this book. I did not know I had it in me until you pulled it out. Thank you for the oil that never runs dry.

To my amazing husband Malachi for your never-ending love, support, motivation and absolute marketing genius. I could not have asked for a better person to share my life with than you.

To Wayne Malcolm for being the first official life coach figure in my life at a time when I thought it was all a gimmick. Hearing you week in and week out for the last eight years enormously helped to awaken the giant within me.

To Len Allen for planting the seed in me that a book can indeed be written in seven days, and then being gracious enough to coach me through it. It was at one of your seminars that I received the profound revelation that writing a book is not just for smart people, it is for anyone who has thoughts to express – and I have plenty so this is the first of many!

To Goretti and the City Business Library team for hosting my very first '7 Keys to a Successful CV' seminar and all the subsequent ones. Thank you for your gracious support.

To all the people that entrusted me with their CVs, cover letters and application forms over the years, allowing me to grow in confidence, experience and expertise in this area. Thank you, I could not have written this book without you.

Foreword

At the time of writing, there are 2.43 million unemployed people in the UK chasing 450,000 jobs. On average, five or more applicants are now competing for each vacancy. How are you going to beat the competition?

When the supply of talent in the labour market outweighs demand, standing out from the crowd is essential. A CV that communicates your unique attributes to an employer is the difference between securing your ideal job or not – it really is that simple. Think you can fill in the gaps and tell recruiters the interesting stuff when you meet face to face? Think again.

Recently, a friend of mine (a Group HR Director of one of the UK's largest retail businesses) ran an advertising campaign to recruit 250 new positions. To her utter dismay her team received 75,000 applications within a fortnight. Ouch. That's a lot of CVs. As you can imagine, it's hard work screening 75,000 job applications (no matter how big you are) which is why her initial short-listing process was based on recruiters spending 30-120 seconds scanning the key points of a CV. Two weeks later, 73,500 people had been told "thanks but no thanks" on the strength of their CV alone. First impressions count.

> *"Find a job you love, never do another day of work in your life."*
>
> **Confucius**

We all deserve to be happy. Sometimes we've just got to give ourselves a helping hand, especially when it comes to self-promotion. Mildred's book will give you that helping hand. These strategies and tactics will increase your chances of getting that job if you follow the seven keys closely.

Mildred's career saw her spending time on both sides of the recruitment fence and several years on the 'front-line' whilst running CV workshops. The experience she shares in this book provides a unique insight into what makes recruiters 'tick'. Despite having spent 20 years helping hundreds of employers recruit tens of thousands of people, when I read the manuscript I even had a couple of "penny dropping" moments myself!

This book will help you work out where you want to go, what you have to offer, and help you stand out from the crowd – even in a competitive recruitment process. Remember, your CV is one of the most important pieces of self-promotion you'll ever create. It can be a passport to wherever you want to go or the barrier, so give it the thought and attention it deserves.

So read the book, go find the job you deserve, and have some fun. And start now, after all, there's another four people out there already after your ideal job.

Good luck!

Richard Tyrie

Co-founder of GoodPeople & Jobsgopublic.com, Trustee of social enterprise charity UnLtd.

Preface

Six years ago I applied for a job as an editorial assistant at a small film magazine. I had recently graduated with a creative writing and film studies degree and was keen to get away from the Saturday library assistant job I was currently in and into the media where my real passion was.

I sent in my carefully crafted CV which highlighted my relevant media experience (all of it unpaid) and a well-written cover letter. One week later I handed in my resignation and took up my new role at the magazine. Within three months I was promoted to assistant editor and it was in this role that my journey into CV writing began. As well as the regular duties of a magazine editor (generating content, commissioning writers, liaising with designers, printers and so on), I was given the task of recruiting new staff members and work experience candidates, which meant that I came into contact with a *lot* of CVs.

I literally went through hundreds of CVs over the course of two years and what I found most shocking was the evident lack of preparation that went into this incredibly important document. Tiny font sizes, serial underlining, overuse of italics, too many pages, too little information, bad grammar, spelling mistakes, missing dates, wrong industry…the mistakes were endless! I had no choice but to reject CV after CV after CV. So much potential was lost and so much talent went unseen all because of a failure to accurately communicate on paper.

This got me thinking that despite all the information available on the internet, at job centres, and other career advice places, there were still people struggling to create good CVs. I realised there was a gap in the market for good quality CV writing and advice, so I said goodbye to the magazine and set up as a CV consultant. Since that day I have gone on to help hundreds of people with their CVs through one-to-one sessions, seminars and workshops.

I believe that writing a good CV is a skill that can be learnt. While there are no magic formulas that you can apply or wand that you can wave to automatically get you an interview, there are 7 fundamental keys to a CV that works, and I will be sharing them with you in this book. You will particularly benefit if you are a student or graduate new to the job market, or you are returning to work after a long absence or redundancy. My hope is that reading this book will not only help you create a CV that works, but more importantly it will be the first step towards obtaining a fulfilling work life for yourself.

To your career success.

Mildred
June 2011

Introduction

What is a CV?

'CV' is an abbreviation of 'curriculum vitae', which is Latin for 'course of life'. A CV is essentially a document that charts the course of your life – more specifically, your work life – for the purpose of gaining employment.

It is what you, the candidate, present to a potential employer in order to be considered for employment within his or her organisation. As such a CV can be considered your passport to a job interview and just like the real thing, it is important to make sure this document reflects you at your best and that it is always kept up to date for when the need arises.

Your CV gives the employer an insight into who you are as a person so it is crucial that you give yourself the best chance possible by investing time and effort into creating a CV that works.

A sales tool

One important thing to understand about your CV is that it is a sales tool. Your CV is your own personal advert which affords you the opportunity to "sell" yourself to a potential employer. Imagine you are a dress or a suit in a clothes rack full of other dresses and suits – how would you stand out to the buyer? What makes you different from the pack? If you can really grab this concept and run with it, you will find it a whole lot easier to create your CV as the process then becomes all about showcasing your very best side to the employer. You are also competing against other "sales people" so your CV must convince the employer that if they choose you, you will be able to generate a significant return on investment, to borrow a sales term.

What employers look for

A lot of people make the mistake of thinking that their CV is all about them – wrong! It is all about the employer and what you can offer them. Every industry is different as is every employer, but what they all have in common when going through CV applications is that they are all looking for a specific set of skills, experience and personal attributes which they have deemed necessary to perform that particular job. If you can effectively demonstrate these three values in your CV, you are putting yourself in very good stead to be shortlisted for interview.

A typical employer would whittle down the number of applicants by listing each candidate against the essential requirements of the job and shortlisting only those that meet all the essential criteria. Where there are too many potential candidates, the next step is to refine the shortlist even further by matching those who also possess desirable qualities the employer is also looking for. This is why it is very important that you include as much relevant information as possible on your CV as related to your field. We will talk about this in more detail later.

Every word counts

The key to writing a good CV is to make every word count – there should be no word on your CV that does not have a purpose or lend itself towards your overall vision of getting your next job in your chosen field. The best way to use this book is to have your CV open in front of you (or a blank piece of paper or screen if you are starting from scratch) as you go through the book. You might want to do this over a seven-day period, taking one key a day, or blitz straight through it all in one afternoon. Whatever you decide, once you correctly apply all the keys in this book, what you will end up with is a CV that works for you.

The 7 Keys

The following seven keys are based on my own experience of creating successful CVs for many people over the years, as well as broader research on what employers look for in a CV. These keys are the building blocks upon which every effective CV is based.

Key 1.

Know Your Target

Before you even think about writing a CV, you must first know 'who' you are targeting, otherwise you are simply playing Russian roulette with your work life. This key is foundational to creating a CV that works; without this key, none of the other six will have meaning or purpose.

Talk the talk

This first key has two important components – the first is about knowing who you are and your own wants and desires in relation to your career; the second is about knowing your potential employer and what they are looking for from a future employee.

Every industry has its own language, merits system and pathway so for your CV to work you need to be able to speak the same language as your chosen industry. What might impress in one field may do the complete opposite in another – a graphic design degree may be just what a marketing director needs to fill the last slot in his team, but for the customer services manager in a retail shop, it is of no benefit to how many shoes you can sell in one shift!

It is important that you demonstrate early on how relevant you are to the role by speaking the same language. Have a look at this extract from a job advert for a web developer, posted by a digital communications agency:

> "We are looking for an exceptional individual to become our Web Developer and work within our enthusiastic team. The successful candidate should possess excellent knowledge of XHTML, CSS, Javascript and PHP. An understanding of HTML5, CSS3, mobile platforms and server administration (Linux/LAMP) will be an advantage."

Most people outside the IT industry would have no clue where to start in deciphering the meaning of this advert, but clearly XHTML, CSS and the rest are standard vocabulary in this sector. If you are to have a better chance of securing your next job, you need to know the vocabulary of your target market and use it effectively on your CV.

Make it relevant

Employers can be understandably brutal when it comes to filling a vacancy. A busy employer with scores of CVs to sift through does not have the time to go through irrelevant CVs – they are only looking to interview those candidates who most closely match their needs, so applicants who do not meet the basic requirements for the job are quickly eliminated.

Targeting your CV simply means that you tailor everything on your CV to your chosen industry in a way that is clearly visible. The skills, experiences and achievements you highlight on your CV must be relevant to the industry you wish to work in. If you want a job as a visual merchandiser in a retail shop, for example, everything on your CV has to say and demonstrate your love for clothes and fashion. On the other hand, it is no use highlighting your great sales experience if the position you want is in accounting; rather you should highlight any financial skills, achievements, relevant qualifications, memberships and anything else you have that relates to numbers. This can include experience in bookkeeping, exceptional spreadsheet skills or an ACCA membership – all these must be immediately visible on your CV.

Making sure that your CV is tailored to the position you are applying for shows that you have a good understanding of what the employer is looking for, which will undoubtedly work to your advantage.

Generic CVs do not work!

In case you have heard any different, here is the truth – generic CVs simply do not work! It is incredibly unwise to have a "one CV fits all" approach to your job hunting if you are at all serious about making advancements in your career. Employers can spot generic CVs at a glance – they are usually the ones littered with phrases like, "I am looking for a job in a challenging and rewarding environment" (more on this when we talk about personal statements) – and they do not like it. They think "you don't want *this* job, you want *a* job" so these CVs tend to be among the first to hit the rejection pile.

You absolutely need to know what industry you want to work for and have an idea of the type of job you would like before you even begin to create a CV. Imagine trying to have a meaningful one-to-one conversation with four people all at the same time; pretty difficult, isn't it? In the same way, sending out a CV that is not targeted is job-seeking suicide, or at best, a waste of precious time.

People put out generic CVs for two main reasons: laziness or varying job interests. If you create a generic CV out of laziness it simply shows that you are not bothered about the company or their job and evidently have not made any effort for it. If this is the case, can you really expect a reasonable employer to give you an interview, let alone a job? Most employers are spoilt for choice with every vacancy so you really cannot afford to be lazy on your CV.

Multiple interests, multiple CVs

The second category of generic CVs is a lot easier to cure. If you find that you have multiple interests, skills, and experience in various fields, instead of creating a generic CV that does not work, what you need is multiple CVs with each CV tailored to each of your chosen industries.

Remember, once you have created your targeted CV or CVs, you can use it again and again to apply for different jobs within that same industry without having to change your CV each time – a good CV really is for life!

 TIP: Create more than one CV if you have more than one interest – each CV must be uniquely tailored to the industry.

Summary

- Generic CVs do not work
- Every industry has its own language and merits system
- Know your industry and tailor your CV to it

Action point

 Decide on the job industry you want to apply for. Spend 45 minutes to an hour researching this industry online (**prospects.ac.uk** is a good place to start) and look at the following:

1. The types of roles available;
2. The skills required for the job;
3. The length of necessary experience;

4.   Any particular qualifications specified;

5.   The vocabulary used in the relevant job adverts.

Jot down some notes on the common factors of your industry and how you can incorporate the requirements and language on your CV.

Young jobseekers

 This is the best time of your life job wise because it is the time for you to experiment with different things before deciding on what you like. At this point you may not know what jobs you would like so targeting your CV can be difficult.

However, there is one way around this: if, for example, you decide you want a Saturday job in a retail shop, think about what kind of items you want to be selling – would it be women's clothes, men's, trainers, shoes, accessories, or mobile phones? What you then have to do is demonstrate your interest and any relevant skills you have in this area in your introduction (see Key 2) and in your interests and activities section – what you do in your spare time. So, for example, if you wanted to work in a phone shop you could say, "I enjoy finding out about the latest phone gadgets. I have an iPhone and I often download the latest apps to keep up-to-date with trends."

If you cannot think of anything that demonstrates your interest in the job you are applying for, chances are this might be the wrong job for you anyway so you are probably better off looking elsewhere.

Key 2.
Get In Order

Now that you have your target in mind, the second key to a CV that works is all about the order – what goes where. The way you arrange the information on your CV should have a nice flow to it, like a good novel or film which tells a continuous story that flows well from beginning to end.

There are three main types of layouts for arranging CVs: chronological, qualifications-based, and the functional or skills-based CV.

1. Chronological CV

With a chronological CV, the emphasis is on your work history and your career progression, therefore everything is listed in reverse date order, i.e. the most recent information first. This usually works best when you have had continuous employment in the same industry with no gaps in between. It can also be good for letting the employer see immediately what you are currently up to, saving them the trouble of searching it out.

On the downside, this type of CV leaves little room for personality and may put you at a disadvantage if your most recent employment or achievement is neither the most relevant to the job or your strongest point. For this reason, this type of CV is particularly bad for people who wish to change careers, but good for those who wish to demonstrate continued career progression over the years.

2. Qualifications-based CV

As the name suggests, a qualifications-based CV is all about your academic achievements so the focus is on education over work history. This type of CV is suitable for students, recent graduates, postgraduates, or people with little or no formal work experience in their chosen sector.

It is also most useful in specific industries such as medicine, IT, finance or social work, where certain qualifications are a mandate for the job. Structuring your CV in this way allows the employer to immediately see that you meet the necessary academic requirements for the job which is valued more than the practical experience.

A word of caution however: in a difficult economic climate, it is not enough to just list your grades (no matter how high) on your CV and expect an influx of interviews to come your way. When employers are spoilt for choice even those who value educational achievements as a key criteria for the job also look for people who also have practical life experience that can support the theory. It is important that even if you are using this type of CV, you still find a way to present your key skills in a visible and direct way.

3. Functional/skills-based CV

This third type of CV is referred to as "functional" because it directs the employer's attention towards a person's functional capabilities (what you can do) as opposed to other aspects of the CV. It is the most targeted of all three CV types in that it emphasises the abilities, achievements and expertise you have that are in direct relation to the

> **TIP:** A skills-based CV allows you to give more weight to your voluntary or unpaid work experience, which is great for new job entrants or career-changers.

industry or job you have chosen to target. It brings together your collective skills both from your employment and other activities and presents them in a way that immediately showcases your strengths and causes the most impact.

The skills-based CV was previously most used by people with little or no work experience or mature candidates seeking to move careers, but with the increasing competition in recruitment, the trend of using this type of CV has risen dramatically over the last few years. It is important for the employer to be able to see straightaway that you have the key competencies needed for the job and using this CV layout allows you to easily highlight your overall and transferable skills immediately. I would recommend this form of CV for most people, except where your industry is one of the exceptions previously mentioned.

What does a good CV layout look like?

Using the skills-based model, a typical good layout for a CV would look something like this:

ERIK JOHAN

T: 020 1234 5678/M: 07951 234 567
121 John Smith Avenue, London NW1
E: erikjohan@madeupeemailaddress.com

Personal Profile

Highly motivated individual with over ten years retail management experience in luxury fashion and an excellent track record in sales and leadership.

Key Skills

* Excellent verbal and written communication;
* Problem-solving and budget handling;
* Leadership and management.

(Significant Achievements)

> Awarded best performing retail manager for five consecutive years;
> Contributed over £500,000 worth of sales to Anonymous Department Store within three years of taking over the management.

Career History (& Voluntary Work)

Manager – Anonymous Department Store, London – Jul 06-Jan 11
Oversee all store operations including managing a staff team of 20 and developing and implementing plans to maximise sales and meet set goals and objectives.

Education & Training

BA (Hons) Management Studies – Top University, London – Sep 01-Jun 04
A-Levels in English, Business Studies and Science – Top College, London – Sep 99-Jun 01

Interests, activities & memberships

I enjoy shopping, travelling and reading, and I am also keen on sailing and running marathons.

Page header

The only thing that should be written at the top of your CV is your first name and surname in big bold letters, not the words curriculum vitae! This is a classic mistake that many people unfortunately still make today, particularly when copying ready-made templates from questionable online CV websites. You can be rest assured that the employer will know what a CV is when he or she sees it so there is absolutely no need for a reminder. This vital space should be reserved for your name – the one thing you want in the employer's mind after your CV has been read!

Your name should be directly followed by your full contact details – home telephone number, mobile, email address, and postal address. If you have a blog or personal website that is relevant to your industry, include the address here also. It all goes towards making you stand out in a crowded market.

 TIP: Unless the job specifically asks for it, never put your salary details on your CV – this can put you at a disadvantage if your previous salary is too high as it may disqualify you for the job; or if the salary is too low, you might undersell yourself, missing out on extra pay.

Personal profile

This section of the CV is very important as it is the introduction of your CV. What you say here determines whether the rest of the content is worth reading; more on this in the next key.

Key skills

Many people make the mistake of putting this crucial section on page two, or worse still, missing it out completely! This is where you really get to sell yourself to the employer so it is incredibly important. We will cover key skills in more detail later.

(Significant achievements)

This section is in brackets – and therefore optional – so not everyone will need to have it on their CV. This is the section where you literally SHOUT about any impressive achievements or accolades you have gained in your work or personal life. This can be anything from winning the best customer service award in your team, to single-handedly bringing in £100,000 worth of sales as a medical rep for three years in a row, or being promoted to a managerial or executive role within your firm. Remember, your CV is a sales tool and you are competing against other candidates so there is no room for shyness and false modesty.

Career history

This is where you list all your relevant employment to date in reverse chronological order (i.e. the most recent first). This section should back up the skills you have outlined in your key skills section and any significant achievements you have mentioned. This should not be a list of tasks and descriptions of your day-to-day responsibilities within your role, but rather a well-thought out demonstration of your experience, the impact you have made in your previous roles (achievements) and your career progression to date.

This is where you really focus on the benefits you have added to your workplace in occupying your role. Think about your actions and how they have impacted on other staff members, customers, or the organisation as a whole in any way. Perhaps you increased the company's profits, reduced costs, increased efficiency, trained others, implemented new procedures, installed new systems, tackled waste…whatever the case, write down the key benefits in several bullet points. It is important to show your potential employer what you are capable of doing for them should they employ you.

Your career history section should look something like this:

Administrator
FYI Research Ltd, London NW1 **Jun 08-Mar 11**

Carried out a number of administrative duties including setting up distribution lists, producing certificates and updating spreadsheets, diary management and coordinating a customer survey;

Arranged meetings and events, scheduling, identifying and being aware of who should attend and where necessary, making arrangements for them to do so;

Suggested and organised fundraising events including a cake sales day and a Valentine's Day disco, fully adhering to Health and Safety procedures.

TIP: Only list the month and year of your current and previous employment. It is always better to put the dates on the far right of the page (your job title and place of work are more important details and therefore deserve the prime positioning of the left hand), particularly where you have career gaps you do not want to draw particular attention to.

You can call this section of your CV employment history but avoid calling it work experience as that carries connotations of an inexperienced student. Where you have carried out voluntary work that is directly related to your chosen industry, you can include this within this section simply puting the word "voluntary" in brackets after the job title to indicate its nature. All other voluntary work should be mentioned in your interests and activities or completely left out of your CV.

Education and training

This is where you list your education and any relevant training or courses you have done to support your career to date. You do not need to include your secondary school or college education if you are a mature applicant. If you are a young person, you need to state not only your secondary school or college education, but also the grades you achieved.

Interests, activities and memberships

Some people debate whether or not this section of the CV is necessary to include at all; I would definitely say that it is. This is the place where you can give yourself a slight edge over other candidates by listing any interests, activities or memberships you have that are relevant to your

TIP: Only include genuine interests and activities on your CV otherwise you could end up the star of a very embarrassing scene at the interview stage.

field but you have not had the opportunity to mention elsewhere. For example, if you are the chairman of your local youth club on a voluntary basis, this is a key role for applying for managerial jobs therefore it is good to include it here (or within the career section under voluntary jobs, depending on how formal the appointment is).

Also, whereas the rest of your CV is pretty much about your work life, in this section you have the opportunity to inject some of your personality, to show a little bit of who you are outside of work. Avoid listing "watching movies, keeping fit and socialising with friends" as your only interest – not only is this incredibly generic, it also does not offer much information about you as a person so it is simply more redundant words. If you need to say this, make it as specific as possible, for example:

> "I am a big fan of kung-fu movies, with over 200 Jackie Chan films in my collection. I regularly go to the gym to exercise and I take part in the London marathon every year. I have an active social life and enjoy going to the theatre and to motivational seminars with friends."

Always include things which you have excelled at, for example, running marathons, winning your local public speaking championship, being made a board member at your children's school, and so on. If you have an unusual hobby that you find is usually a conversation starter, include this here. I once gave a CV makeover to a lady whose hobby was to collect and sell Persian carpets. Not only was this an interesting hobby, it actually said a lot about her as a person, as well as the kind of skills she was likely to possess as a result. Unusual interests or achievements can help you stand out and be more memorable, as well as provide a good talking point at the interview stage. Remember, your CV gives the employer a first impression of who you are so think carefully about the image you would like to leave them with.

What about references?

I have deliberately left out references and even the popular statement, "references available on request" for two reasons: first, employers ask for references anyway and do not need reminding to do so; secondly, when they do require a reference, it is in almost every case after the interview stage of the process where they have decided to offer you the job. Mentioning references at all is therefore a waste of precious CV space.

Summary

- Your CV should have a nice flow to it, like a well-written novel.

- There are three types of CV layouts: chronological, qualifications-based and functional or skills-based.

- The skills-based CV is the best choice for most people.

- A typical good order for a CV is as follows: Name and surname page header, contact details, personal profile, key skills, significant achievements (optional), career history and voluntary work (optional), education and training, interests, activities and memberships.

Action point

- Carefully go through your work history; think about any significant achievements you may have overlooked and pull these out on their own.

- Arrange your career history section in reverse chronological order. For each role list at least 3-4 bullet points on the impact you have made. Include dates started and ended in months and years only, and the general location, e.g. London.

Give more attention (and therefore space) to jobs that are similar to the one you are applying for. For jobs that are beyond a 10-year period and not directly relevant to the role you are applying for, only give limited details such as your job title, name of employer, dates, location and your main responsibility.

Young jobseekers

I would recommend a mix between the skills-based and the qualifications CVs. To supplement your lack of experience you will need to pull out things you learnt in education that will support your application. So for example, you can demonstrate how good you are at working under pressure and keeping to deadlines by talking about the coursework assignments you had to hand in and the exams you had to sit – and pass. These are valid ways to gain these skills.

Your interests and activities will also help you so pay particular attention to this section. If you have held any roles of responsibility, such as being a school mentor, or maybe you performed a solo piece at your end of year assembly or got the highest grade in your whole school for a science coursework, or any other thing like that, list these under your key achievements.

Key 3.

Engage Your Intro

In business, this section of your CV would be referred to as your elevator pitch, based on the American concept. It works like this: imagine you just entered a lift on the ground floor and the top executive of your dream company walks in behind you. You are both going all the way up to the 10th floor and there is no one else in the lift. This is it; this is the opportunity you have been hoping for. You have thirty seconds to make an impression and hope that he hires you for that dream job. So…what do you say?

In a similar way, most employers make a decision on whether your CV is worth reading or not within the first thirty seconds of laying eyes on it. What you say in the opening section of your CV can make all the difference to how far you progress in your application.

The introduction section of your CV – otherwise known as your 'personal statement' or 'personal profile' – is where you summarise who you are and what you have done in the most impactful way you possibly can. Think of it like the trailer to a movie, or the blurb on the back of the book – if the little clip you see or the short amount of text you read does not engage you sufficiently, chances are you will not bother to watch the film or read the book. You want to make sure that what you write in your intro is so powerful that it grabs the employer's attention and causes him or her to read on.

What you call it matters

Whilst it is okay to call this section 'Personal Statement' or 'Personal Profile', avoid calling it 'Career Objective' at all costs. The simple reason for this is that your career objective is for you to know and not your employer. To put it quite bluntly, the employer does not care about what *you* want in a career, rather they are concerned with what you can do for *them* in their company should they offer you the role. Remove all mentions of your career goals or aspirations on your CV – the only exception to this would be young jobseekers (see below for more details). If you target your CV well, abiding by the seven keys in this book, you will be able to make a statement about your career objectives without spelling it out in black and white.

So what's in a good intro?

A good personal profile section literally summarises who you are, what you have done and what skills you possess in no more than two to three sentences! You need to be original; avoid using generic terms and clichés and make it as specific as possible to your personal attributes. If you have a particular qualification that is a basic or even desirable requirement for the job (for example, 'Prince 2' for a project management role), mention this straightaway in your intro – the idea is to put forward your best attributes as quickly as possible, bearing in mind that you only have thirty seconds to make your impact before the lift hits the 10th floor!

The good, the bad and the ugly

The best way to illustrate what to do and what not to do in your personal profile is by showing you some genuine examples, starting with the **ugly**:

> "A highly motivated sales consultant with a resourceful personality and expediential experience in sales and customer service. Possesses excellent communication skills and has highly developed analytical and interpersonal attributes needed to excel in business."

At first glance, the above intro does not seem so bad, does it? But beneath the surface are lurking lots of ugly errors:

> "A highly motivated <u>sales consultant</u> with a <u>resourceful personality</u> and expediential experience in <u>sales and customer service</u>. Possesses excellent communication skills and has <u>highly developed analytical and interpersonal attributes</u> needed to <u>excel in business</u>."

- **Crime 1: Labelling**
  This person starts off by calling themselves a "sales consultant" – this limits you to one job title and unless this is the exact job title you are going for, you immediately disqualify yourself from the race. A better way would be to say, "A highly motivated sales professional".

- **Crime 2: Keyword overuse**
  This intro is absolutely littered with 'killer buzzwords' that literally mean nothing in this context – "*resourceful personality*", "*expediential* experience in sales", "highly developed *analytical and interpersonal attributes*". One or two of these is fine when used in context and personalised to who you are, but to literally stuff your intro with words like this lacks a personal touch and immediately points to a generic CV.

- **Crime 3: Mixed targeting**

  The mention of business in the last line of the CV is confusing – this person either wants a job in sales or in business, it cannot be both. Yes it can be argued that sales is business but a sales consultant on the shop floor is hardly going to experience the business side of things so that knocks that argument to the ground. Generic CVs (as this one is) go for a catch-all approach and unfortunately miss all in the process.

 TIP: When using keywords in your introduction, aim for descriptive and informative words such as creative and analytical which lend themselves to describing skill and character attributes. Follow on where possible with an example that qualifies their usage.

Overall this intro does not reveal anything substantial about this person that can be used in their favour. A better intro would be:

- "Highly motivated individual with great communication skills derived from a sales and customer services background. Creative problem-solver with an outgoing and approachable personality and a willing attitude to hard work."

So you have seen the ugly, now here is an example of a **bad** intro:

- "Having recently completed a business degree, I am currently seeking full-time employment within the marketing sector. I feel that my adaptability to change and my conscientious approach to clientele situations makes me a viable candidate for this type of career."

Were you able to identify any of the reasons that make this intro bad? Here is the answer:

> "Having recently completed a business degree, <u>I am currently seeking</u> full-time employment <u>within the marketing sector</u>. <u>I feel that</u> my <u>adaptability to change</u> and my <u>conscientious</u>

approded <u>approach to clientele situations</u> makes me a viable candidate for <u>this type of career</u>."

- **Crime 1: Stating career objective**

  This candidate starts by mentioning the type of employment they are "currently seeking". As we already discussed, it is never a good idea to verbally state your career objectives in your CV. If you have targeted your CV well enough by following the first key, your whole CV will literally shout out your career goals without you having to formally mention it. Remember, your career goals are for you to know and not the employer.

- **Crime 2: Self-focus**

  It is important to remember that your CV is *about* you but not *for* you. Therefore, all subjective references such as "I feel that…" must be either quantified, or better still, removed completely. From the number of 'I's, me's and my's' in this intro, it is evident that this person is self-focused and has not taken enough time to consider what the employer wants.

 TIP: Always refer to yourself in the 'third person' on your CV. So instead of "I am a talented individual…", a better alternative is "Bob is a talented individual…" Even better still, remove the pronouns completely, so in this case the sentence would just start with "Talented individual…"

- **Crime 3: Meaningless words**

  Similar to the ugly example, this person makes use of jargon which carries no particular meaning. With their "adaptability to change" and "conscientious approach to clientele situations", you would need an English interpretation dictionary just to figure out what this person is trying to say! People sometimes make the mistake of thinking that the more "big words" they include on their CV, the more intelligent it makes them sound; this is simply not the case. It is far better to make sense using simple straightforward language than to write nonsense in big words.

- **Crime 4: Commitment warning bells**

  The phrase "I am currently seeking" is a very bad one to use in your intro for the simple fact that it implies a general broad search for a job. This is made worse still by the additional mentions of employment "within the marketing sector" and "this type of career". All of these sound warning bells to an employer – it says that this candidate is looking for *any* job they can get, which ultimately means that if I (as the employer) give them the job, invest my time, effort and money in training them, and another company comes along and offers them a better role or more pay (as evidently this type of candidate continuously applies without much targeting), then all that time and money I would have spent on them would have been in vain. This is a risk that no employer wants to take so this CV is very likely to hit the rejection pile very quickly.

A much better intro would be:

> "Business Studies graduate with theoretical and practical experience in sales and marketing gained through university and internships with companies including Penguin Group and Sainsburys Ltd. Flexible and hardworking with great initiative and the ability to work efficiently to deadlines."

And finally, the 'poster boy' of intros – the **good**:

> "Enthusiastic and creative self-starter with five years proven experience in media production, working with some of the key players in the industry including ITV and Endemol UK. Efficient, focused and driven with strong research and events management skills developed in a commercial environment."

This is as close to as perfect an intro as you can get for this very simple reason: in just two sentences and less than 50 words, this person has managed to communicate their personal attributes ("enthusiastic and creative self-starter"), relevant experience (number of years, key industry players), knowledge of the industry (commercial environment), and the key skills that they possess. In addition, they have also utilised a very useful tool in CV writing – name-dropping.

Name-dropping

This person mentions two of the key industry players he or she has worked with in the past. Although name-dropping may be frowned upon in social settings, on your CV it is perfectly acceptable – in fact, more than that, it is a *must* if you are truly serious about selling yourself!

Working with major 'brand name' employers in your field and mentioning it on your CV is like having a particularly good work reference; in some cases, it may even be the very thing that gives you the edge over other candidates and lands you an interview. These name brand employers do not have to be paid work either. Whilst starting out in my media career I did work experience at a few places including some brand names – the *Daily Mirror* and the *Guardian* newspapers. On two occasions after starting a new job where I got through on my CV, I have had my new employer say to me that seeing those names on my CV really swung the boat for them – they simply *had* to call me in for an interview.

Just as we talked about in the first key, every industry will have its own brand names so if you have worked for some big names that are relevant in your industry, mention it straightaway in your intro – do not make the employer have to scan all the way down the page to your career history to pick up this crucial information as they may not even get that far.

Presenting your experience

It is important to understand that the good intro is not just good because the person has former experience that works to their advantage; if you read the ugly intro again you will see that this person also has former experience in their field but the skill is in communicating it well – this is what makes the crucial difference.

You can certainly still have a good intro even if you do not have a lengthy work history and that is where work experience and voluntary roles can really come in useful to give you added credibility. Here's an example:

> "Communications Masters student with international journalism and PR experience gained in France and London. Creative, outgoing and hardworking with good interaction skills and a passion for challenging and rewarding projects."

Remember, your CV is a sales tool and you are the product so it is your responsibility to sell yourself to the best of your ability to stand the best chance of getting the job you want.

Summary

- Your intro is like the trailer to a movie or a book blurb – it must be engaging enough to grab the attention of the employer and make him or her want to read on;

- Do not write any more than 2-3 sentences in which you summarise who you are, what you have done and what skills you possess;

- Lose the self-focus and write your intro in the third person;

- Avoid using 'buzzwords' and putting in any words or information that you cannot back up in the rest of your CV.

Action point

 Write your own strong introduction, bearing in mind the good and bad examples shown above. Start by writing down all the important information you think will sell you instantly, no matter how long, and then go back and edit it down until you are left with no more than three average length sentences at the most.

Young jobseekers

The only exception to the "do not mention career objective" rule applies to you. When you are new to the job market without much work experience under your belt, it is a good idea to include a career objective at this stage so that the employer knows where you are going in life.

However, do not say things like, "I want to progress in your wonderful organisation" – this sort of information is for the cover letter. Rather, talk very briefly about your overall ambitions; for example, if you are applying for a sales assistant role in a sports shop, your career objective could be:

> "My goal is to become a manager of a successful sports shop within the next five to ten years."

Also mention your educational achievements and, as we already talked about, the strongest of your key achievements could form your CV intro. Here is a good example of an intro for a young jobseeker going for an IT apprentice position:

> "Motivated and hard-working young man with a passion for IT and a natural skill for fixing computers. Quick and adaptable learner with good insight and the ability to analyse problems and come up with solutions."

Key 4.

Reveal Your Skill

Okay, you now know who you are targeting, you have structured the order of your CV and you have created a super-engaging intro – now it is time to reveal your skill to the employer! At this point you already have a good chance of getting an interview so keep on going.

What exactly is a 'skill'?

The *Oxford English Dictionary* defines skill as "the ability to do something well" – an expertise or a particular ability. A skill, in essence, is something that you are good at, whether naturally or developed by training.

This section of your CV is particularly crucial because here is where you present to the employer what you are bringing to the table, so to speak. It is where the employer asks, "Do you have what I am looking for?" and with a well-presented CV, your answer will be "Yes!"

Drawing out your work skills

Practically everything we do at work involves using a skill of some sort but often we are blissfully unaware of this. Take for example a receptionist at a front desk: the phone rings and she answers politely (communication); while she is resolving that query, a courier comes to deliver a parcel which she signs for, supporting the phone with her neck (multitasking). No sooner is she finished than the chief executive comes down to announce an urgent meeting at midday and requests an immediate room booking (dealing with pressure). She checks through the online system, finds a room and makes the booking (basic IT and administration) and then heads over to the room at a quiet moment to prepare it for the meeting (customer service, organisation).

We can go on with this scenario but I think you get the point. The same is true of your own work life – you possess a lot more skills than you have probably given yourself credit for on your CV so really putting this key into practice will help you to redress that balance.

TIP: Have a notepad (or a Word document) at work where you keep a record of all new tasks you perform, skills you gain, challenges you overcome and achievements you secure. Write down what you did, when and the outcomes. You can then easily transfer this information to your CV when the time comes.

Other sources of skills

The good news is that your skill does not have to come from just your career or paid work experience, it can literally come from anywhere. In his management book '*Successful Recruitment and Interviewing*', Dr Rob Yeung advises:

"Relevant experience [of using a skill] may not always have come from doing paid work. A candidate may have experience of using a skill from their charity work, community groups, sporting pursuits, studies, and so on."

The extracurricular activities we do not only demonstrate self-motivation and passion, but often they also equip us with highly desirable skills such as teamwork, leadership, organisation, administration and much more.

One key area in particular that people tend to miss out on their CV is their role in a religious organisation. I have come across many people who hold significant positions at their local church, mosque, or other worship centre, but are afraid to put this information in their CV at the risk of religious discrimination or appearing as a 'fanatic'. The question you need to ask yourself is, "Is my role here relevant in any way to the job I want to get?" If your answer is yes, do not leave this information out of your CV. You can either present the information in your career history section as a voluntary job, or you can list the skill in your key skills section, for example, committee leadership skills, and then specify your role as a church/mosque leadership committee member in your interests and activities section.

By this point the employer would have been so taken by you already that they would hardly let something like this put them off! Besides, you have the law on your side – under the Equality Act 2010 employers cannot discriminate against potential employees on the grounds of religion as well as race, gender, age and much more. If you suspect discrimination as a reason for not getting shortlisted for an interview (although bear in mind that this can be difficult to prove), you can get help from a number of agencies, including the government website **www.direct.gov.uk**.

How do I know which skills to put down?

Employers want to see skills and qualities that match their selection criteria for the job so the simplest answer to this is that it depends on what the job requires. Once you have carried out Key 1 and researched your target market, you should have a pretty good idea what is required in your industry so these are the skills you need to present on your CV.

It is a good idea to have an overall look at your current and past roles, responsibilities, achievements, and your interests and activities outside of work to pull together your key skills section. Include skills that are directly relevant to your industry, general soft skills such as communication and time management, common transferable skills such as multitasking and organisation, computer skills, and any technical skills you may possess.

Top transferable skills

1. Communication (verbal and written)
2. Planning and organising
3. Research and administration
4. Teamwork
5. Multitasking
6. Leadership and management
7. Time management
8. Problem-solving and initiative
9. Adaptability and flexibility
10. Computer literacy

Presenting your skills

When using the skills-based CV format, your skills are best presented in short bullet point summaries. You can separate your 'soft skills' from your technical or industry-specific skills (if applicable). What you are looking to achieve here is short, direct sentences that explain the skill and provides evidence to back it up. Here are a few examples of good skill statements, presented in a two-column layout:

- Experienced in forging strong partnerships with decision makers and stakeholders from public, private and voluntary sectors.

- Excellent communication skills with fluency in five languages, including French and German.

- Consistent problem-solving ability derived from customer services background.

- Able to strategically plan, develop and deliver successful engagement projects and programmes.

- Strong verbal and written communication skills demonstrated by prior experience producing reports and delivering presentations to groups of various sizes.

- Computer literate with a good grasp of Microsoft Office packages and a typing speed of 45wpm.

Using job adverts and role profiles as an aid

Job adverts are very good for picking out skills because they list the skills right there in front of you in the language of the employer, as you can see in the following example:

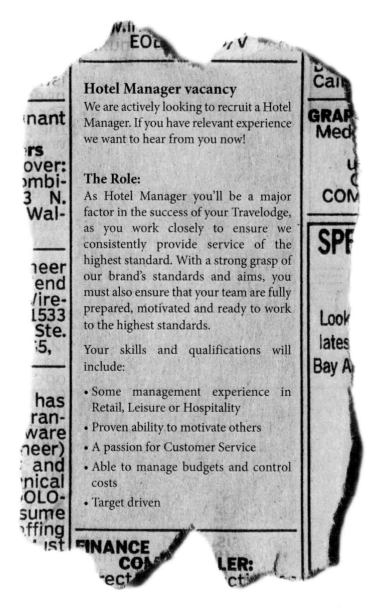

Hotel Manager vacancy

We are actively looking to recruit a Hotel Manager. If you have relevant experience we want to hear from you now!

The Role:

As Hotel Manager you'll be a major factor in the success of your Travelodge, as you work closely to ensure we consistently provide service of the highest standard. With a strong grasp of our brand's standards and aims, you must also ensure that your team are fully prepared, motivated and ready to work to the highest standards.

Your skills and qualifications will include:

• Some management experience in Retail, Leisure or Hospitality
• Proven ability to motivate others
• A passion for Customer Service
• Able to manage budgets and control costs
• Target driven

Another useful tool for pulling out skills is the role profile for your current or last job. This is good because it actually has sections about the skills and competencies required for the job and as you are or have been in that role, you should now be able to match up to the skills outlined so you can literally carry out a cross-referencing exercise.

Use both of these as an aid but do not simply transfer the requirements outlined in a job advert to your CV because any discerning employer will be able to see through that straightaway, causing your plagiarised CV to meet the rejection pile. Remember, everything you put on your CV must be truthful to you and backed up by evidence. If you somehow manage to get away with making empty claims on your CV, you might find yourself in the uncomfortable position of turning up to an interview and not having any real answers or examples to relay in the questions you are asked.

Summary

- Your skill does not have to come from employment alone – it can be from community or voluntary work, studies, sporting pursuits and other activities.

- Job adverts are useful tools for picking out and identifying skills, but do not copy them word for word.

- Clearly distinguish your soft skills from any technical or industry-specific skills you need for the job.

- The more skills you have, the more attractive you become to an employer so do not be afraid to get more skills where you need it.

Action point

Play out an average day at your current or last job in your mind. Think about every task and how you carry it out and pick out the skills involved. If you are able to, you may find it easier to take a notepad in to work one day and make a conscious effort to observe everything you do and write down every skill involved.

Think about your extracurricular activities, memberships, community or voluntary work you may do. What skills can you pick out from these?

Young jobseekers

We pick up a lot of skills that we are often not aware of, right from a young age. Any skill you can demonstrate in this section will be to your advantage. Have a go at writing down everything you can think of that you are good at – think about the things your friends, family, teachers, or even strangers point out about you and write them down. Use the chart below to figure out how it translates into a skill and write this on your CV.

Personality	Possible skills
You are a friendly person who is very good at making friends.	Communication, relationship building, networking
You are tidy and organised and like things in order.	Administration, organisation, presentation (written)
You talk a lot and find it easy to get your point across.	Communication, presentation (verbal)
You write everything down whether it is letters, poetry, short stories, or even text messages. You keep a diary or have an online blog.	Written communication, note-taking, secretarial, administration
You know how to get people together to do something; you are usually the one giving orders.	Leadership, management, organisation, decision-making
You are good at coming up with solutions for things. You enjoy solving puzzles and difficult scenarios, and often play crosswords and Sudoku.	Problem-solving, numeracy, methodical, logical
You like working in groups and enjoy sharing your own knowledge and learning from other people.	Teamwork, flexibility
You are happiest working on your own because that is how you best get things done.	Initiative, resourcefulness

Key 5.

Looks Can Kill

You have heard the saying that beauty is in the eye of the beholder, right? Well that does not apply to CVs! The way your CV looks is just as important as the content – after all, what good is it having great content that's badly presented? Just ask a chef!

A poorly presented CV can kill your chances of getting an interview even when you are the best candidate for the job so it is very important that while you take the time to work on your content, you also give just as much attention to the appearance. Do you have to be a graphic designer to pull this off? Absolutely not! We are not talking about design skills here, just good professional presentation and there are a few rules about this.

A discussion on fonts

You may have previously come across the terms 'serif' and 'sans serif' in the discussion of fonts and wondered what they were all about. Without boring you with too much unnecessary detail, the basic difference is that serif fonts – like Times New Roman,

Georgia, `Courier` and Sabon – have small lines towards the end of the characters (called 'serifs') and sans serif fonts – such as Arial, Tahoma and Helvetica – are without these lines.

An old-fashioned font instantly dates your CV and gives the impression that it has not been updated for years. Times New Roman is a classic example of what *not* to use. When people first started word processing CVs in the days when computers first came about, Times New Roman and Arial were among the early fonts, which automatically made them the preferred ones. Whilst Arial has managed to remain relevant through time (though there is not much longer to go until it too becomes old-fashioned), the same cannot be said of Times New Roman so avoid using this at all costs.

Many new fonts have come in to play since then so there are now lots of choices available. I would recommend using fonts from the sans family where possible as they tend to be cleaner, clearer and more modern than the serif fonts. They also look larger in the same point size compared to the serifs, which makes them the better option for CV writing. I would recommend Verdana, Tahoma, or fonts similar to these but steer clear of Comic Sans as it comes across as childish and unprofessional which is not the statement you want to be making on your CV.

You may want to deviate in your headers to create visual variety, but try not to use more than two different fonts throughout, otherwise your CV will look messy and unprofessional. Also be mindful that some computers may not have the same capabilities as yours so stay away from obscure fonts which may display correctly on your PC but have an altogether different appearance on your potential employer's, distorting the entire look and feel of your original document. The best way to ensure this does not happen is to also create a PDF version of your CV and use this in your job applications instead of the Word version. PDF readers are available on pretty much all computer platforms so your CV can be viewed in exactly the same layout and format you created it. Most modern versions of Microsoft Word contain a PDF export function but if you do not have one on your PC, you can download a free PDF converter from various websites.

Size matters

The CV font size was more of an issue in the days when applications were sent by post or printed and hand-delivered to a local store. The advent of the internet, and with it online job applications, means that you can afford to be a bit more flexible with sizing as there is the option to zoom in and out when viewing on screen.

However, as most employers tend to print out the CVs before reading, I would advise sticking to the following conventional boundaries: sizes 10 or 11 generally work well for the body text to allow for easy reading without the crude appearance of text that is too big for purpose. Your subheadings should be one or two sizes larger than your body text and bold, and the main page header should really stand out – I recommend at least a font size 22 for this purpose.

 TIP: When sending your CV as an email attachment, make sure to include your first and last name in the document's name, for example "CV – Sally Somebody.doc". This makes life a whole lot easier for the busy employer or HR assistant who often has to sift through and file scores of electronic CVs for every job vacancy.

Employing visual aids

It is important to have clear differentiators for each part of your CV to allow the employer to find specific areas quickly and easily. While this can be achieved with a simple line break, bullet points, bold formatting, and columns are excellent visual aids when used correctly.

Bullet points help to create concise sentences for emphasis, making your CV easily scannable by the employer – important when time

TIP: Use bullet points and columns to break up the text for better visual display.

is short. They are quick and easy to read, and look attractive on the page, as long as you do not have too many of them. Bold formatting is great for distinguishing subheadings and important points, but for even greater distinction in subheadings, employ bold with a different font from the main body text. Columns are a useful way of saving and creating space all at the same time. A great way to use columns is in the key skills section to break up the monotony of listing point after point (see example in Key 4) but try not to break it up into more than two or three columns, otherwise it becomes visually distasteful.

Applying visual aids correctly gives the employer strong visual signals about how the CV should be read and helps with the flow of information.

Avoid unnecessary styling

Do not get carried away with style applications – I have seen CVs where pretty much everything has been written in italics and believe me, this is a struggle to read through in one go. Italics used on a one-off basis or very minimally is fine, but when overdone it can be very hard to read and a busy employer is not likely to have the time, desire or patience to follow through with this mammoth task.

The same caution applies to underlining and using bold formatting. The purpose of both of these is to draw particular attention to a point or to distinguish a word, sentence, or section from another. When overused it totally defeats the purpose, causes unnecessary chaos and confusion and crucially looks unprofessional. Finally, shadow formatting on a CV is a big no-go area, so too is decorative borders, head to toe use of coloured text, fancy typefaces and any form of image – including your passport picture!

Allow room to breathe

Space is an important factor in the looks department. You must leave plenty of white "breathing" space on your CV as well as generous margins on all sides. Resist the urge to cram a word or extra styling wherever you can – too much writing on a page can make your CV appear cluttered and hard to read.

 TIP: Write your full name as a footnote on every page to remind the employer whose CV they are reading and in case the pages of your CV get separated for any reason. It is also worth including a contact number here for easy reference.

Be consistent

Once you have chosen the style and format of your CV, this should remain the same throughout, including fonts used, heading size and arrangement of text. Tabs are useful tools to employ, but when using these be sure to keep the positioning uniform throughout.

The right tool for the job

Make sure your CV matches the industry sector you are going for. If you are in the creative industry, for example, you have liberty to be a lot more creative with your CV than someone in, say, finance. Sometimes you may even want to add a hint of coloured text to further improve the look and give you visual advantage over other competitors. But again everything in moderation, so while a deep red header here and there may work, writing the whole CV in blood red may not go down too well with your potential employer.

Where the paper matters

If you find yourself in the increasingly rare position of having to send your CV by post, print it on plain good quality white paper, adhering to the same font and style guidelines above. Unless you are applying for a design job which requires you to demonstrate creativity, there is no need to print your CV on coloured paper, embossed paper, or anything else of that variation.

Only print on one side of an A4 paper for better presentation and just in case the employer forgets to photocopy both sides.

Summary

- Your CV will be judged on how it looks just as much as the content so it is important you present it in the best way possible.

- Choose the right font and keep the size readable.

- Keep the finish clean, professional and skimable.

- Employ the use of visual aids to help you with the presentation.

Action point

- Experiment with the font of your CV to make it as clean, clear and modern as possible.

- Experiment with some style applications.

- Think about your industry and what would be acceptable in context. If there is room for creativity, try experimenting with a bit of colour and a more unconventional layout.

Young jobseekers

As this might be your first or one of your first CVs, the employer will not be expecting it to be amazing so this is your chance to really wow them with your presentation. Be a little bit creative – but not too much as it should still be professional – and maybe add some colour, depending on the type of job you are going for.

Feel free to think outside the box – at a recent CV seminar for a class of 15-16 year olds, one of the students asked me if it was okay to write your CV by hand to stand out from everyone else. I said, "Absolutely – if you have the time, patience and a neat enough handwriting for such labour!"

One lady shared with me her experience of applying for a work experience placement at a very popular radio station with a word-processed CV and a handwritten cover letter some years ago. She confessed that she only hand-wrote the cover letter because she did not have access to a home PC at the time and the closing date was fast approaching. Much to her delight she got the placement over hundreds of other applicants and when she started the office manager shared with her that the handwritten cover letter was what swung it for her as it demonstrated a level of dedication and a personal touch that stood out above everyone else.

So there you have it – a success story of using unconventional methods! I am not saying that you should do what this lady did but as you begin to think creatively around your job hunting, you are bound to come up with innovative ways that will distinguish your CV and separate you from the crowd.

Key 6.

Check It Out

This key is all about attention to detail. One of the most ironic things I have ever come across on a CV is someone claiming to have "great attention to detail" in their key skills section and then proceeding to litter the rest of the CV with typos, spelling and grammatical mistakes!

What's so bad about a few typos?

Admittedly, even the most stringent of news desks on a national paper with a football-sized team of subeditors can slip through a typo now and again, but your CV is far too important a document to run such a risk – particularly as first impressions count and that first impression is the only chance you have to make your mark.

Would you turn up to a job interview in dirty, crumpled clothes with uncombed hair? The same thing applies for your CV. Employers consistently list typos, spelling and grammar mistakes as their biggest turn-off on a CV. A CV with errors speaks volumes to the employer – it says that if this candidate cannot make the effort to eliminate errors on their CV, how can we guarantee that he or she won't employ the same lazy, slapdash approach to their work? This may sound harsh and may be as far from the truth as it can ever be, but that's the way that perceptions go so it is well worth doing all you can to eliminate this problem.

 TIP: Print out your CV when going through it for errors – it is far easier to spot mistakes on paper than it is on screen, particularly when you have been staring at the same document for any length of time.

There is no excuse

There really is no excuse for bad spelling or grammar in this day and age with so many resources available to help; also, the average CV is only two or three A4 sides at the most, therefore it is a relatively short document and should not demand much time to pay close attention in this area. It is vital that you proofread your CV after you have finished and once you have done so, hand it over to someone else to read through as a fresh pair of eyes can more than likely spot the things you may have missed out, particularly if you have been staring at the computer screen all day.

You may also want to consider hiring a professional editor to go through your CV for you so that you can have complete and utter peace of mind.

Check the spelling

By all means use your computer's spellchecker as a starting point, but do not let it end there. Spellcheckers can be prone to mistakes and misspellings of their own and they are unable to pick up common errors such as writing 'form' instead of 'from', or 'your' instead of 'you're'.

Also beware of Americanised spellings (mainly substituting 's' for 'z') if you are applying for jobs in the UK – this is still considered a spelling error.

TIP: Make sure your computer spellchecker is set to UK English. If in doubt of the alternative spelling offered, look up the word online in a UK-set search engine and see what result comes up from reputable sources (like national newspapers).

Use punctuation correctly

Pay close attention to punctuation when going through the checking process. There is so much to look out for but as a general guideline make

TIP: Keep a dictionary nearby to double-check anything you're unsure about. You might want to have a thesaurus too for added vocabulary.

sure you have full stops at the end of every sentence and use commas and semi-colons (where appropriate) as 'pauses' to break up long sentences and different words. Where possible make your sentences no more than a line and half long or approximately 15-20 words.

If you use brackets or quotes, remember to open and close them accordingly. Do not use exclamation marks on your CV for any reason – there is hardly ever a reason for such excitement, save that for the interview!!! Watch out for your use of capital letters, making sure that this is consistent throughout.

Employers create shortlists with one simple objective in mind – to make the potential list of candidates short. No matter how innocent a spelling mistake, grammar error or typo may seem, it can make your CV (and as such, you) appear unprofessional and can literally be the thing that keeps you from making the shortlist, no matter how great your overall application.

Summary

- Spelling and grammar mistakes on a CV are highly unprofessional and give the impression of a lazy candidate with poor attention to detail.

- Do not over-rely on your computer for spellchecking, it cannot pick up everything.

- Always get a second pair of eyes to look over your CV, if possible someone who is a professional in this area.

Action point

Go through your CV thoroughly on paper a day or so after you have finished the first draft. Find a quiet place and go through each line with a red pen in hand, ready to catch any rogue errors that may have slipped through.

Read it out loud very slowly, one word at a time, to make sure it makes sense throughout.

Try changing the look of your CV by temporarily altering the size, spacing or style of text. This may trick your brain into thinking that it is seeing a new document which can help you get a different perspective on what you have written.

Young jobseekers

A more common problem employers are finding with young jobseekers is the use of 'text' language on CVs. Where it is perfectly okay to use slang and shorten words in a text message to your friend, doing the same thing on your CV is a major crime that can cost you the job.

Try and get an older or more experienced person to look over your CV once you have finished. I would recommend a teacher or a careers advisor unless you have a parent or older brother or sister who is particularly good at these things. You can also get guidance and support with your CV from various youth organisations, details of which can be found on the **direct.gov.uk** website.

Key 7.

Sell, Don't Suffocate!

If you have followed the six keys correctly, by this point your CV should now read brilliantly and look great. You would have discovered how incredibly employable you are as a person and how much you have to offer in terms of your knowledge, skills and experience – you should be feeling pretty confident of your job chances by now.

This final key is where you apply some brakes to make sure you do not go overboard. It can be very tempting to include everything you have ever done in your life, but remember your CV is just a snapshot – your very best snapshot nonetheless – that shows who you are and what you have to offer to the employer. The sole aim of your CV is to sell yourself just enough for the employer to invite you in for an interview; after that the job is yours if you play your cards right. As an aside, a former manager once revealed to me that if an employer calls you for an interview, it means they want to give you the job so all you have to concentrate on is bringing to life the person on the CV. This little piece of information gave me confidence to approach interviews time and time again after that and I hope it does the same for you too.

Ditch the irrelevant info

In order to really sell yourself on your CV, you need to ditch any information that does not lend itself to your career objective. We already talked about dropping "references available on request" but there are other space wasters to avoid. This includes any mention of your age, date of birth, sex, religion, marital status, physical characteristics, passport number, driving licence (unless you are applying for roles that require regular driving such as a lorry driver or an estate agent), number of kids, political preferences, or any other personal detail that has no bearing to your quest for employment.

Also leave out your expected salary, reason for leaving your last job, and any past failures or health problems (it is not necessary to disclose the latter except where it may directly affect your ability to perform the job, in which case you should declare this at the interview stage).

Not only are these irrelevant at this stage of your job hunting process, on a more serious note they can potentially be used as a basis for discrimination. A potential employer will only spend seconds glancing at your CV before deciding whether it is worth reading or binning so keep your CV relevant and informative.

As an aside, do not be tempted to tell lies on your CV or even stretch the truth – you may be able to get your foot in the door this way but you will be found out somewhere along the line. Besides, I can think of few better ways to ruin the experience of starting a new job or career than being haunted by the fear that your little white lie may come to the surface some day.

Keep it fresh

It is important to keep your CV updated with details of any new roles you take on at work, awards or accolades you receive, skills you pick up, courses you complete, or anything else you learn along the way that can lend itself to boosting your credibility in your chosen industry. The best thing to do is to jot down the details as soon as it happens because while it is still fresh in your memory you can really capture your key tasks and achievements in a way that best sells you.

As you add new information, go over the old to make sure that everything on your CV is still relevant and still directed towards your career goals. Remove anything that is no longer relevant – or "go quiet" on it (see FAQ section) – so that your CV can maintain its freshness and relevance.

Having an up-to-date, ready-to-send CV is critical to your job success. But even if you have decided you never want to work another day in your life for someone else, maintaining the habit of keeping your CV up-to-date is good because it can help you to keep track of your own career and achievements, which can sometimes be difficult to remember accurately in hindsight. Also, the information you write on your CV is transferable and can be used on your business plan, personal website, or even your LinkedIn social profile.

 TIP: Refresh your CV at least once every 3 to 6 months, even if you are not looking for a job. This is to help you keep track of your career progression, and also to always be ready in case your circumstances suddenly change.

The question of length

There is sometimes much unnecessary debate over how long a CV should be. The truth is the length of your CV actually depends on how much you have to say – in other words, the length of your career history, educational background and your general life experience. A student or recent graduate may have just one page whereas someone with a twenty-year work history may have three. However, two A4 pages is generally accepted as a good length for a CV because it gives you enough room to say all you have to say without overdoing it.

There are a few exceptions to the rule: technical and academic (research-based) CVs tend to require more space, as do people with longer work history and those going for very senior or executive positions. However, if you have correctly applied the first six keys and still find that you need a little bit more than two pages to really communicate all that you have to say, take it! It is better for your CV to spill over to a third page and still be readable than for you to suffocate it into two.

Make sure that you have been ruthless in your editing of information and only include what is absolutely necessary and relevant to the particular industry you want to apply for. Remember, you can always create multiple CVs if you have more than one area of expertise or interest.

Summary

- Resist the temptation to include everything you have ever done in your life on your CV.

- Remember your aim is to sell not suffocate, so avoid making your CV too long.

- Two pages is best for CVs, with a few exceptions.

- Be ruthless in your editing and lose any unnecessary information.

Action point

- Go over your CV again thoroughly and for each statement, bullet point or sentence, ask yourself if it is absolutely relevant and whether it contributes to the overall goal of getting the job you want in the field you have chosen.

- If you have not already done so by this point, hand over your CV to someone you trust. Get them to take on the role of your potential employer and role play with you, asking you questions about the content of your CV and the job that is being advertised. Use this exercise as a way to make sure you have adequately covered all the key points needed.

- Be open to constructive criticism on all aspects of your CV.

- Set yourself a target to go over your CV once a month and see if there is any new information you can add or old information you can take away.

Young jobseekers

It is perfectly okay for you to have a one-page CV – in fact this is probably the length yours will come to if you do it properly. As you progress in your career it will get more detailed as you develop more knowledge, skill and experience.

You can include your GCSE and A-level results but you do not have to list each and every grade, so do not worry about being embarrassed if your grades are not all A stars. You can simply put the total number of GCSEs or A-levels you have, the grade range, and any key grades you want to draw particular attention to, for example, 9 GCSE A-Cs including B in Maths and C in English.

A Note on Cover Letters

Now that we have gone through the seven keys to a CV that works, it is time to look at something that is equally as important to the job-hunting process – your cover letter.

Cover letters

In ninety-nine per cent of cases where a CV is required for a job, a cover letter is also required. Even if it is not explicitly asked for, it is good practice for you to send one anyway. A cover letter is your CV's best friend. Where your CV decides whether or not you are called for an interview, a cover letter decides whether or not your CV gets a look in at all, so it is incredibly important.

In the old days, cover letters were literally that – letters you sent in the post as a cover for your CV. It still has the same function today, except with online applications a cover letter can be written in the body of an email with a CV attachment as opposed to being a separate document. However, to make life easier for the employer (remember, this whole process is all about them), it is a good idea to *also* attach your cover letter as well as putting it in the body of the email – this way, if they want to print out your application or pass it around the organisation, it is nice and straightforward to do so.

Your cover letter serves as the bridge between the job advertised and your CV, and as such should be no more than three-quarters of an A4 page. The letter introduces your CV and your CV backs up the facts you talk about in the letter, as well as providing further details of other supporting material. How you accurately translate information on your cover letter can give the employer a hint about your suitability to the job.

Still in the sales business

By now you should have it firmly in your mind that getting your next job is all about sales, therefore your cover letter should effectively sell your CV. If your cover letter is bad, the employer is highly unlikely to waste his or her time reading your CV – it literally can make the difference between success and failure in your job search.

Do not make this mistake

Once you have applied the seven keys to your CV, you will have a CV you can use over and over again without having to alter it with each application. A cover letter, however, is the opposite – this *must* be changed with every application and must be tailored to the job you are applying for.

The biggest mistake you can make is to send out generic cover letters. As an employer I have had cover letters sent to me addressed to the wrong person and, worse still, the wrong company; needless to say, these went straight into the recycling bin! Every employer would like to think that anyone applying to work for their company would be there for the long run to help strengthen the business, so just like the awful non-targeted intro we talked about earlier, a generic cover letter has implications of a candidate continually up for sale to the highest bidder – no employer wants this for their organisation.

Presentation still counts

Your cover letter should match your CV in font and format, particularly when sent by post, but also by email. Apply the same rules of font size, paragraph spacing, bold for effect and so on. Up-to-date email editors will allow you to edit the text in HTML which allows for Word-like formatting.

Structuring your cover letter

If you are sending your cover letter by post, you should start with your full name and address in the top right hand corner of the page (see reference section for samples), followed by the date, and then the employer's full name, job title and address on the left hand side of the page. After this comes your greeting, the job title as the reference, and then the main body of the text, followed by a closing salutation and your name below, leaving a space of about three or four lines for your signature (this adds extra professionalism). The same structure applies for a cover letter by email except you lose the addresses, date and signature space when copying and pasting directly into the body of the email.

 TIP: You can create an electronic version of your signature either by writing it clearly on paper and scanning it into your computer, or by making use of an online site that offers signature-creation services (a quick search should reveal some of these).

What's in a name?

Where possible address your cover letter to an actual person as opposed to "Dear HR" or "Dear Sir/Madam", as it personalises your application. Some job adverts give you the name and job title of a particular contact to reply to, but where a name has not been supplied, this is your chance to show a little initiative and score some brownie points for yourself. You can either research the information online on the company's website, or you can call the relevant department of the organisation, tell them the job you are applying for and politely ask who would be the best person to address your cover letter to. If they are unable to provide you with a direct contact, you have not lost out on anything, but if they do, you have just given yourself a slight edge in the job competition.

When you are using a name, make sure you get the correct name and that you spell it correctly. If it is a woman and you are not sure whether she is a 'Mrs' or 'Ms', don't write either; instead use 'Dear first name surname'. It might sound insignificant but a married woman addressed as 'Ms' may find it offensive which might get you off to an unnecessary bad start.

Your opening statement

A good way to think of the cover letter is like a longer version of the intro (personal statement) of your CV. Once you have correctly addressed your potential employer, the next thing to do is tell them what you want and why you want it. This is where you talk about the position on offer and what attracted you to it. Keep it simple, relevant and to the point, making sure it is clear what position you are applying for (particularly important where the organisation has a number of vacancies). A good opening statement might say something like this:

> "I would like to apply for the Media Executive role which I saw advertised on your website. I am passionate and experienced in the media and would like to continue to grow in this area. I believe that working for <company name> in this role is just what I need to achieve this."

Unlike the CV, you can afford to be a bit more subjective in your cover letter where the language is concerned. Avoid being overly formal, instead aim for a friendly, yet respectful style to build rapport with the employer and encourage them to read your CV. Once you have got 'you' out of the way in your opening statement, the rest of your cover letter goes back to focus on the employer, demonstrating why you are right for the job but still maintaining the same friendly-formal tone.

The main body

This is where you address your key strengths, qualifications, experience and anything else that makes you exceptionally suitable for the role, according to the job description. Remember this is a prelude to your CV and you only have three-quarters of a page at most so only include *key* information in no more than two paragraphs.

The best way to approach this is to play the matching game. This is where you take a few of the key criteria the employer is looking for and pair it with evidence from your CV. So let us say, for example, that you have a marketing degree, some paid experience in marketing and basic work experience in PR and you come across this advert:

> "We are looking for a Marketing and PR Assistant for a three-month internship. You will be assisting our Marketing and PR coordinator with online and offline support of marketing initiatives, supporting the PR agencies with information and visuals, compiling reports, uploading info on both our websites and assisting with social media.
>
> The successful candidate will have a degree in marketing or media, excellent organisational and office skills, excellent verbal and written English, a passion for beauty and a strong work ethic."

Already you can see there are lots of things to pick out for your main body. So taking it line by line, you can mention your marketing degree in the intro and then move on to address their requirements. Ask yourself questions about every criteria: do you have experience of online and/or offline marketing initiatives? Have you worked with PR agencies before? How good are you with visuals and compiling reports? Have you had to upload to websites before, even in your own personal time? Are you active in social media – do you use Facebook, Twitter and the rest? Can you demonstrate organisational skills? Do you have office experience? Are you passionate about beauty? Do you have evidence to support this passion?

There are literally lots and lots of questions you can ask yourself around the job description to stimulate answers you can turn into sentences for your cover letter. You do not have to match every single requirement of the job (if you do, you may want to consider applying for a more challenging role!), but you do need to demonstrate how you match as many of them as possible, particularly the most important ones.

Final words

Once you have finished the main body, it's time to summarise and again remind the employer how keen you are about the job, as well as inform them of your availability for interview and when you could start, should you be successful. Thank them for their time in reading your application and include your phone number for quick reference.

TIP: Sometimes it may be appropriate (usually for speculative applications) to demonstrate your willingness to be proactive by initiating follow-up in your closing paragraph. You can do this by letting the employer know that you will contact them in a week or two (be specific) to discuss your application and hopefully look at setting up an interview date.

Your closing salutation should be formal, polite and professional, such as Yours Sincerely, Kindest Regards or Best Regards. Do not simply sign off with Thanks as this is too casual and unprofessional.

Finally, do not forget to proofread your letter very carefully for spelling and grammar errors and any typos that may have sneaked through.

Summary

- Always address your cover letter to a real person whenever possible.

- Spell that person's name correctly and check the company details.

- Make it presentable – try and match it to your CV if printed.

- Do not write more than three-quarters of an A4 page.

Action points

- Write your cover letter in response to the significant points of the job description.

- Find a fresh pair of eyes to read it for spelling and grammar mistakes but also to see how well it covers the main points of the job.

Young jobseekers

Your cover letter is just as important as your CV so make sure that this is specific to the job you are applying for. If, for example, you want to work in Topshop, ask yourself, why this particular shop? What attracted you to Foot Locker instead of Sportsdirect, and Carphone Warehouse instead of T-Mobile? Answer these questions first in your mind and then on paper in your cover letter.

Even if your aim in getting a job is *just* to get some money, would you really do *anything* for money? If that was the case would you apply for a cleaning job right now? If your answer is "No way!" then it means that there is a reason you are applying for this particular job, so think about it properly and write that reason down.

.

Frequently Asked Questions

Q: Do I have to put my date of birth on my CV?

Absolutely not. The Employment Equality (Age) Regulations 2006 made age discrimination illegal in the recruitment process which means that, in theory, you should not be turned down for a job because of your age, thus eradicating the need to include your date of birth.

Q: Do I have to include my home address on my CV?

Your home address is part of the basic information the employer needs to know about you (alongside your name and contact details) but increasingly more and more people are citing identity fraud as a reason to leave this out of their CVs. Although identity fraud is a valid concern – particularly when submitting CVs to online sites – the actual occurrences of this happening are nowhere near enough to justify omitting your address totally.

A full address should always be included in direct applications (ones that go straight to the employer or a reputable agency) but when posting your CV on a public or semi-public forum, it is sufficient to just put your town and city – for example, "Dagenham, London".

Knowing where you live helps the employer determine how close you are to the office and how long your potential commute would be – this is useful information that can be the deciding factor between two strong candidates. Additionally, missing out your address can appear suspicious and raise unnecessary questions about your credibility.

Q: Should I include a picture on my CV?

Unless you are looking for a job in acting, modelling, TV presenting and the like (in which case you will have a completely different CV anyway), you should never include a photo on your CV except where the employer specifically requests it. Yes, there is a very slim chance that having a photo could work in your favour if you look like a movie star, but for everybody else it could become a point of unnecessary distraction or discrimination. The rules differ outside the UK so if you are looking to work abroad, it is a good idea to check what the conventions are in your chosen country.

Q: My first name is ambiguous – people often do not know if I am a man or woman on paper; how do I address this on my CV?

If you have a gender-neutral name or an unusual name from which it is difficult to determine gender, there are two ways around this: you can either include your middle name if that is more gender-specific, or you can put your title in small brackets after your full name – for example, Aubrey Jones (Mr).

Q: How far back do I go in my career history?

As far back as you need to go to illustrate how relevant you are to the job you are applying for, but bear in mind Key 7 and be sure to sell, not suffocate. If you find that your most relevant accomplishments are in your most recent positions, then up to ten years is generally fine. If it is a real mixed bag with some recent and some in the past (usually occurs when people are returning to a particular field of work) the way around this is to be "loud" on the relevant ones and "quiet" on the others, no matter where they are located on the CV. So, for example, you would write two sentences and several bullet points about the position where you want to be loud, and just one sentence to summarise where you want to be quiet. If you have been working for a good number of years, you can usually leave out some of your very early roles without any real consequence.

Q: How do I tackle gaps in my career history?

If you have been in employment for any length of time, it is perfectly natural and acceptable to have gaps of a few months here and there from being out of work – most employers understand and are sympathetic to this. However, if you find that your gaps are closer to years than months, do not try to hide this – you are going to need to explain what you were doing during this time (whether on your CV on in an interview) and the best policy to adopt is honesty, particularly where you have a legitimate reason such as a study break or having a child.

If your gap was a deliberate career break where you spent time travelling and exploring the world, mention this explicitly in your employment history section, stating the start and end date and listing a few relevant experiences you had or lessons you learnt along the way. If your gap was as a result of being made redundant in your last job, it is best to mention this as early as possible – I would recommend in your intro – and then use the rest of your CV to demonstrate how brilliant you are! Seriously, once you get this information out in the open, you can confidently move on with the rest of your CV without the need to specifically address the gap. Also, redundancy is usually something that is out of your control so most employers will not necessarily view this in a negative light.

If the gap was for a health reason you have now recovered from, it is best to leave this information out of your CV completely to avoid being overlooked unnecessarily. You can then be honest about it at the interview stage, explaining that it is no longer an issue and therefore will not affect your ability to carry out the required work.

Whatever the reason for your gap, try and find the most positive aspect in the situation and emphasise this on your CV. As tempting as it is not to mention those lost months or years, it is much worse to leave them out all together because if you do the employer will have no choice but to guess what should be there – and nine times out of ten their guess would probably be worse than the truth.

Conclusion

Putting in all this time and effort might seem like a lot of work, but the good news is once you have a CV that works, you are pretty much set for life. All you have to do is refresh it regularly to make sure it is up-to-date and still in alignment with your career goals and objectives and you are good to go.

Finding your next job

It is important to remember that people get jobs in many ways, so alongside the more common routes of applying for an advertised job or going through an agency, consider being proactive by approaching a number of organisations you would like to work for and offer yourself in a particular role – the worst case scenario is that they either say no (in which case your details are now with them anyway in case anything comes up) or you do not hear back from them at all. On the other hand this method shows great initiative and literally sets you apart from the competition so it could very well work in your favour.

Who you know can also play a part in getting your next job so extend your network of friends and acquaintances and let people know you are looking. Utilise modern technology in your job search – join LinkedIn, Facebook, Twitter and similar social networks to raise your profile and connect with people in your chosen industry. The more methods you employ in your job search, the more likely you are to succeed.

Sample CVs and cover letters

All of us have different skills, interests and experiences which must be communicated uniquely for best results. I would encourage you to only use these samples as a *guideline* to creating your very own bespoke CV and cover letters.

CV sample 1

Erik Johan
creative & versatile designer

Mobile: 07900 123 456
Email: erikjohan@madeupeemailaddress.com
Address: 7 Keys Drive, Longbridge, London KE7 7KY

personal profile:
Creative and versatile designer with excellent understanding of digital design principles and standards-based web and graphic designs. Accurate and organised with proven experience of delivering high quality results for clients.

technical skills:
Adobe Flash | Dreamweaver | Photoshop | Illustrator | InDesign | Fireworks | HTML | CSS | JavaScript | PHP | MySQL | CMS | Autodesk Maya | Autodesk 3D Studio Max | CorelDraw | Final Cut Pro | Ulead Video Studio | PowerPoint | Project | PC and Mac literate.

key skills:
- Good written, verbal and visual communication skills with the ability to produce clear and effective designs according to client brief and requirements;
- Keen awareness of web usability and accessibility issues;
- Strong knowledge and skills of Adobe products to create rich visual designs;
- Experienced in the use of Flash for interactive multimedia designs, websites and CD-ROM;
- Up-to-date knowledge of creating and executing social media campaigns;
- Excellent team player with the ability to build and maintain good working relationships across all levels.

career history:

Media Director (voluntary)   **Oct 10-present**
Longbridge Society – London
Recently appointed as overseer of the society's media activities with responsibilities in graphic design, video production and IT support.

Head of Media (voluntary)   **Sep 09-present**
Longway Support Centre – London
Responsible for shaping, developing and advancing the media outreach of this charitable organisation, creating strategies and solutions for effective promotion across various platforms.
- Produce all graphic design materials including flyers and posters;
- Currently redesigning the website;
- Edit promotional videos publicising the organisation;
- Developed and created Longway's logo and brand identity;
- Set up a team for the creation, monitoring and management of social media accounts such as Facebook and Twitter, and various other online campaigns;
- Instrumental in organising outreach events including an international student exchange programme and Longway's fourth anniversary, held in August 2010.

Page 1 of 2

Freelance Web & Graphic Designer   **Sep 07-present**

Clients: Jailbird Media, Carmichael Media, Northside Educational Trust, City Wide International Assembly **– London**

Assume various freelance roles in the areas of web, graphic and multimedia design, including working with clients to create and construct viable brand identities.

- Designed and produced interactive "yearbooks" on CD ROM containing music, pictures and profiles of students, and other information, using Adobe Flash;
- Created promotional flyers and marketing materials using Photoshop;
- Conceptualised and created logos to client briefs and requirements.

education:

Adobe Certified Associate   **June 2010**

Longbridge University

Certificates: Rich Media Communication using Flash CS4; Web Communication using Dreamweaver CS4; Visual Communication using Photoshop CS4.

MA Digital Media   **Sep 09-Sep 10**

Longbridge University

Modules: Principles of Digital media; Design for the Internet; Principles of Games Design; New Media Management; E-Solutions and Digital Media Applications; 3D Animation for Multimedia.

Certificate in Digital Interactive Multimedia   **Apr-Jun 05**

National Computer Institute (NCI) – Dallas

B.Tech Management Technology (Project Management major) **Sep 01-Apr 07**

Dallas State University

Modules studied: Project Management; Statistics; Management Accounting; Labour Law; Applied Mechanics; Engineering Drawing.

Extra curricular activity: Involved in the forming of the 'Association of Management Technology Students' where I was also elected as the first General Secretary for the 2001/2002 session.

interests & activities:

I enjoy reading, writing, listening to music, learning new things, and generally experimenting with creative design ideas. I also like to teach design skills and have prior experience teaching Adobe Fireworks, Photoshop and Flash at a computer institute in Dallas.

Page 2 of 2

71

CV sample 2

Brenda Smithers

Telephone: 020 1234 5678 **Mobile:** 07900 123 456
Email: brenda_smithers@madeupeemailaddress.co.uk
Address: 7 Keys Drive, Longbridge, London KE7 7KY

Accomplished project coordinator with a track record for driving forward initiatives, government take up campaigns and commercial developments. Innovative in approach with a passion and a commitment to delivering high standards and measurable results.

SKILLS SUMMARY

- Able to strategically plan, develop and deliver successful engagement projects and programmes.
- Strong management skills with the ability to inspire and influence a wide-ranging audience.
- Keen eye for detail; able to identify improvements and develop creative solutions to procedures and work practices.

- Experienced in forging strong partnerships with decision makers and stakeholders from public, private and voluntary sectors.
- Excellent communication, relationship-building and networking skills.
- Results-driven with the ability to meet set targets in a pressurised environment.
- Strong organisational and multitasking skills; able to plan and prioritise workload accordingly.

KEY ACHIEVEMENTS

➢ Successfully coordinated and delivered 'Caring with Confidence', a government initiative designed to engage and empower unpaid carers. [**Longbridge Carers Centre**]
➢ Raised awareness and widened participation for lifelong learning within Longbridge, including engaging with and integrating into the community vulnerable and disadvantaged adults and hard to reach critical groups. [**Longbridge Community College**]
➢ Identified and resolved CRM system errors by simplifying the process by which leads become sales, resulting in a more effective record-making system. [**Longbridge Holdings Ltd**]
➢ Generated sales, media and new business opportunities for a range of SMEs including a local commercial radio station, a nightclub, a health and beauty magazine, a distance learning company and a security firm. [**Freelance**]

CAREER HISTORY

Marketing & Sales Coordinator   Mar 10 – May 10
Longbridge Holdings Ltd (trading as LHTL) – Longbridge, Surrey
Assisted the CEO in shaping, developing and delivering the overall B2B and B2C marketing strategy for this new online education business. Initiated and translated innovative ideas into clear actionable plans resulting in customer sales conversions.

- Implemented AIDA principles in copywriting, re-designing and updating the website, and in producing other promotional literature and correspondence;
- Drove customer acquisition, initiating and proactively seeking out cost effective ways of direct marketing with ROI (such as affiliate schemes, social networks, mail shots, search engine marketing and email lists) to satisfy business objectives;
- Planned distribution of 250,000 leaflets using Mosaic to identify target audiences and knowledge of competitor activity to build brand, services and client base.

- 1 -

Project & Events Manager (Caring with Confidence)   Jul 09 – Nov 09
Longbridge Carers Centre – Dayford, London
Worked closely with Department of Health national team to coordinate the implementation and delivery of 'Caring with Confidence', a national government learning and development initiative designed to empower unpaid carers.

- Delivered presentations to Health and Social Care practitioners and policy officers across London to communicate campaign concept and benefits;
- Informed and engaged the public with the programme through face-to-face talks, events and a leaflet and poster distribution campaign at GP surgeries, community centres and local groups;
- Networked at strategic level to build and develop key stakeholder relationships with NHS, Social Services, PCT's, local councils and voluntary sector agencies across Dayford, Longley, Baxley and Broomley;
- Implemented Service Level Agreements, arranging and setting up learning and development programmes to achieve set targets;
- Organised a local conference to launch and communicate the national campaign to Health and Social Care professionals, making all practical event delivery arrangements including venue, catering, registrations and other administration;
- Worked closely with policy officers and as a member of the Council conference planning committee to strategically plan and implement programmes for carers;
- Oversaw Department of Health database, setting up administrative processes systems and maintaining project documentation.

Management, Training & Business Support (Freelance)   Oct 06 – Jul 09
London
Assumed various freelance management, training & business support roles over a three-year period, having taken voluntary redundancy from a long-term career in education. Roles included training delivery, facilitating in schools, volunteering and fundraising for charity, organising and delivering events, and providing assistance to SMEs in the areas of PR and media relations and maximizing innovation and profitability.

EDUCATION & TRAINING

Department of Health – CwC Facilitator Development Programme	2009
CIEH Level 2 Health & Safety in the Workplace	2008
Time FM Media Sales Training	2008
ICM Diploma in Event Management with PR	2007
Elbenar Hospice Charity Induction / Child Protection	2007
Introduction to Cognitive Behaviour Therapy	2007
Teaching Observation, Support and Supervision	2006
Centre of Excellence – Leadership Matters	2005
Network Training – Working with Challenging Behaviour	2004
Quality Circles, including Customer Care, Marketing and Enrolment	2003
Working with people with disabilities including dyslexia and deaf awareness	2003
Managing Change, Personal and Professional Development	2000
Delivering OCR/RSA Modular Awards	2000
Certificate in Education (FE)	1994

INTERESTS & ACTIVITIES

My interests and activities include country walks, foreign holidays, styling, fashion, and personal and professional development.

- 2 -

73

Sample cover letter (basic)

Dear Name of recruiter,

RE: Public Relation & Journalism Internship

I am very much interested in applying for this position which I believe strongly matches my skills, experience and career aspirations.

My background is in journalism and PR with experience gained both here in London and in Sweden, my country of origin.

In my last role as a PR Assistant for an online tourism group, I carried out various reporting assignments including reviewing hotels, theatres shows and entertainment events. I was responsible for contacting different organisations to arrange the reviews, which gave me good experience in liaising with publicists.

Prior to that, I worked in Sweden as a freelance reporter and arts correspondent for a press agency where I was able to gain lots of writing experience and knowledge of the PR industry.

I would love to work with your company and would welcome the opportunity to meet with you face-to-face to discuss the role further.

Please find attached my current CV with further details about my career to date. I am available for interview and if successful, to start immediately.

Thank you for your time, I look forward to hearing from you.

Warmest Regards,

Erik Johan

Tel: 020 1234 5678

Email: erikjohan@madeupeemailaddress.com

Sample cover letter (advanced)

Dear Name of recruiter,

RE: Programme Executive (external education)

I am very much interested in applying for the above position as I believe it strongly matches my skills, experience and career aspirations.

As you will see from my CV, I am a very experienced project coordinator and programme manager with a diverse career background ranging from Health & Social Care and business to the longest of all, education.

Prior to taking a voluntary redundancy in 2006, I enjoyed a 23-year career in education and lifelong learning in a number of management roles at Longbridge Community College. At this institution I was able to develop and deliver innovative education curriculum for a range of learners, as well as organise and manage events designed to raise the profile of the college and promote its educational opportunities and services.

Another key role I previously held is that of Project & Events Manager at the Longbridge Carers Centre in 2009. Here I was charged with implementing and delivering the 'Caring with Confidence' programme, a national government learning and development initiative designed to empower unpaid carers. I successfully managed to inform and engage the public on the programme through a variety of methods, including organising community events and delivering specific presentation sessions to health and social care professionals to enable them to drive forward the initiative.

Throughout my career it has been vital to build and develop key relationships with stakeholders and forge collaborative working partnerships therefore I am very experienced in working with and communicating effectively with people at all levels. I have recently been made redundant due to the company going into administration so I am very keen to be part of an exciting and dynamic team once again.

Please find attached my current CV with further details about my career to date. I am available for interview and if successful, to start immediately.

Thank you for your time, I look forward to hearing from you.

Warmest Regards,

Brenda Smithers

Tel: 020 1234 5678
Mob: 07900 123 456
Email: brenda_smithers@madeupeemailaddress.co.uk

Index